# C O N T E N T S

Interviewing is an integral part of managing people. Successful interviewing doesn't just happen, it requires planning and preparation. What goes on during the interview is only part of a continuing process.

It may be that to date most of your experience has been on the receiving end. We expect and accept that interviewees can be nervous and worried about the impression they will make. Interviewers often feel the same; after all they are in charge of the process.

The next seven days will give you an insight into the way successful interviews are created as we examine interviewing in detail. The first two days deal with some general guidelines and techniques while the next five outline specific types of interview.

You are more likely to be involved in Sunday to Thursday's interviews. Friday's and Saturday's will occur less often.

| | | |
|---|---|---|
| **Sunday** | – | The four Ps of interviewing |
| **Monday** | – | General skills |
| **Tuesday** | – | Selection and recruitment |
| **Wednesday** | – | Appraisal |
| **Thursday** | – | Coaching |
| **Friday** | – | Counselling |
| **Saturday** | – | Discipline |

# The four Ps of interviewing

Throughout the week we will be considering some of the interviews that you may be conducting as part of your job. Before examining each specific type of interview there are some basic guidelines that relate to interviews in general.

> *The four Ps of interviewing*
> * purpose
> * preparation
> * performance
> * postscripts

The four Ps form a handy structure and foundation for any interview. They will help you to clarify where you want to go with the interview, whether you get there and where to go next.

## Purpose

Before you proceed, it is advisable to think through the purpose of each interview. If it is not obvious to you why you are interviewing someone then you can guarantee it won't be clear to them either. Even when the interview is spontaneous you can still take time between you to check the purpose and whether there is an expected outcome.

*Purpose of the interview*
- why interview?
- clear objectives

*Why interview?*
Memos, letters, tests and reports are fine for disseminating the data one way but an interview provides a dynamic and personal interchange. Whenever you want a flow of information, an interview can be the most effective way of ensuring understanding and a sense of rapport between both parties.

*Clear objectives*
If you don't know where you are going you may well end up somewhere else.

Once you have decided that an interview is the most productive way to proceed then you need to have a clear idea of what you are hoping to achieve from it. This will help you decide what preparation is required, the structure you want to follow and how to assess your level of success afterwards. For example, before an appraisal interview your objectives might be:

*Appraisal – Sue Green*

Objectives
- review year's performance
- Sue's assessment of progress
- possible areas of increased responsibility
- relationships with John and Peter
- training or coaching needs

It is vital to let the interviewee know the objectives too. That way they can prepare appropriately and be clearer about the type of information you require. It is easy to assume that because you have given great thought to your objectives they will also be obvious to the interviewee. Not so! They are not mind readers.

It is also important to check what the interviewee's objectives are if you want the interview to be a truly productive and two-way exchange.

## Preparation

Fail to prepare... Prepare to fail.

Preparation is the key to successful interviewing. This need
not be a lengthy process to be valuable. As you become
more experienced with different interviews you will find
that a pattern of preparation emerges and you will develop
your own formula.

*Self*

You may feel uncertain or nervous about the interview you
are about to hold especially if you are not very practised. It
is worthwhile to reflect briefly how you can talk yourself
into or out of a successful interview.

*Compare...*
- thoughts   I know I'll make a mess of this interview; I
  could never interview as well as Harry.
- feelings   Nervous, uncomfortable, panic,
  inadequate.
- outcome   Dry mouth, stumbling over words,
  incompetent impression, avoid interviews.

*with...*
- thoughts   I've prepared well for this interview; I'm
  developing my own interviewing style.
- feelings   Calm, confident, ready, healthy nerves.
- outcome   Well-paced interview, interviewee
  comfortable, positive impression.

Positive self-talk is recognised as a way of enhancing performance whether it be in an interview or on the sports field. If you can direct your energy away from worrying about a situation and towards effective preparation, then you will be creating opportunities for success. When the interview is not as effective or doesn't go to plan, you can use positive self-talk to assist learning rather than beating yourself up for not being perfect.

Take some steps to relax immediately before the interview. Prepare for success.

*Documentation*
You need to collect and read through a variety of paperwork before the interview. In the case of selection, appraisal, coaching and discipline interviews you will have a good idea of the data required. Make a list of all the documents needed and if time is short you can prioritise your reading.

- What key questions arise from your reading?
- Where do you want to start the interview?
- What evidence is available to support your argument?
- Which areas do you want to focus on?

*Organisation*

The organisational preparation for an interview fits into three categories: interview structure, scene setting and administrative arrangements.

*Interview structure* Having decided the purpose of the interview and reviewed the relevant documentation, the next step is to consider the structure. You can mentally plan or write down your opening words and jot down the stages you intend to follow.

*Interview structure*
- before interview – schedule enough time in your diary; inform interviewee of location; set out interview plan.
- during interview – establish rapport; agree or state objectives, set agenda; stick to the point; develop theme(s); summarise and agree conclusions/actions; plan next step/arrange next interview; close clearly.
- after interview – review the content; review the process; follow up agreed actions.

*Scene setting* The location of the room and the way it is set out can significantly affect the interview process. You will require somewhere quiet, free from interruptions either from the phone or other people and with enough space not to feel cluttered or crowded.

You need to find a balance in the room between distractions like paintings, posters, ostentatious ornaments and 'executive toys' and somewhere too sterile which will be cold and unwelcoming.

If you are holding a panel interview with a number of interviewers you need to set the room out so that the interviewee feels comfortable and unthreatened.

What seating arrangements can you make? Both the formality of the interview and the space available to you may determine this. The room layout is one of the first things the interviewee will notice. It is a good idea for most interviews to place yourself on the same side of the desk as the interviewee. If you have chairs set around a coffee table there is room for you both to have papers and somewhere to put coffee cups. This way there is no barrier between you and the interviewee and no sense of suggesting you are the more important person.

Sitting behind a desk can suggest that you are inaccessible, too busy or even frightened by the interviewee. In some offices you will have no choice about the desk. If this is the case then you should at least make sure the chairs are at the same height and that the desk is free from clutter and distractions.

Smoking is another issue to consider. You should be clear from the start about your own and the company's views.

*Administrative arrangements*

- When is the best time for the interview?
  Late morning/midday if interviewee has to travel.
  End of the day for counselling or discipline.
- How can you block interruptions?
  Transfer the phone and put an 'engaged' or 'do not
  disturb' notice outside the door. Use another office.
- How many interviews should be held in a day?
  If they are going to be longer than 15 minutes,
  should try to stop at six a day. Any more and the
  early ones will be forgotten whilst your performance
  will be impaired in the final ones.

## Performance

You can now go into the interview confident that you have
set clear objectives, read the necessary documentation,
decided the interview structure and set the room out to your
liking. The next step is to manage the interview itself. Think
about the points below.

*Interview style*
A warm and non-threatening opening to the interview will
enhance whatever style you then go on to use. The main
essence of the interview is to establish a rapport with your
interviewee to settle them down. Then you can use one or
more of the following interview styles:

*Joint problem-solving* Here, concentrate on a particular
problem, settle together on a way round it and get the
interviewee's commitment to the agreed goal.

*Tell – listen* Provide the interviewee with relevant information or with your assessment of the situation under discussion, and then listen to their ideas for action.

*Tell – sell* This assumes that you know best! You state the facts and then sell your solution to the interviewee. The danger is that the interviewee will not be committed to your goal.

*Listen – support* There may be no 'solution' in this kind of interview. Your role is to allow the interviewee to work through their concerns and consider different ways of managing them.

*Taking notes*

In most interviews, it is wise to take brief notes to supplement the detailed information that your company requires.

Notes are not recommended for a counselling interview where the emphasis is on confidentiality. In any case, you will want to use all your concentration to listen wholeheartedly to the interviewee.

One of the main problems with notes is the distraction caused by the break in eye contact with the interviewee whilst you are writing.

*Hints for notetaking*
- tell interviewee you're planning to take notes and suggest that they do too
- keep notes short and to the point
- put interviewee's words between quotation marks
- write up notes straight after interview
- note facts not personal information

*Prejudice and bias*
It is crucial to remember that you can make decisions about a person or the outcome of an interview in a very short time. Where that is the case, you need to check whether you are relying on 'instincts' or assumptions rather than the facts. If you are selecting a candidate with whom you will be working closely, it is appropriate to pay attention to your gut feelings about them. You can also consider the source of these responses. The interviewee's appearance, someone else's opinion or the fact they arrived early or late may have influenced you unfairly.

When you are conducting an interview with someone you know well, unsubstantiated information may also be influential. If you are inclined against an interviewee, you only notice interactions that reinforce that view. On the

other hand, a particular piece of work may so impress you
that you only see the positive side of that interviewee when
there might also be areas for improvement. Either way, your
prejudices can lead to an outcome that you predicted and
subconsciously encouraged. Concentrate on the whole
picture not just the parts that impress or disappoint you.

Be wary too of your prejudices landing you in trouble with
racial or sexual discrimination and sexual harassment. Many
companies have their own codes of practice and equal
opportunities training. If you are to be involved in much
interviewing it is advisable to make yourself familiar with
these codes and with the law on such matters.

## Postscripts

The three important post interview activities are: writing up
the notes, following up agreed actions and self-assessment.

*Writing up the notes*
As soon as the interviewee has departed write out your notes in full. This may mean filling in a company form or a record card. Don't leave it until later. Once you are back in the swing of work the notes probably won't make sense.

*Following up agreed actions*
If you have agreed to find some information, talk to a colleague, set up a meeting or contact a client, then start to draw up a plan for yourself. How much time do you need to commit to the action? Who else is involved? When is your deadline? What is your review date?

*Review and self-assessment*
Give yourself time to go back over the interview and assess your performance. Was the outcome satisfactory? Was your preparation appropriate?

*Some self-assessment questions*
- Did I establish a rapport from the start?
- Did I clearly state my agenda and objectives?
- Did we agree a shared agenda and objectives?
- Did I listen fully to their discourse?
- Did I summarise accurately?
- Did I follow my interview plan? If not, was that appropriate?
- Did we reach a consensus for future action?
- Did we both gain from the interview?
- What will I do differently next time?

# General skills

The scene is set, you have thought through the basic objectives and your required outcomes for an interview. Now is the time to consider exactly how you might achieve them. There are a number of general skills that go a long way towards creating an effective interview. Many interviews fail simply because the interviewer has not followed a few basic guidelines.

*Basic interviewing skills*

- active listening
- questions
- body language
- obstacles

## Active listening

This is a key skill in any kind of interview. Effective listening involves a lot more than just not speaking at the same time as someone else; a cardboard cut-out can do that. You have to be active in processing what you hear and responding appropriately. Try using the following skills and you'll see how active listening can be.

*Paraphrasing*
This is a way of restating as accurately as possible what the other person has said; using your own words to show you have been listening and have understood them. It is very helpful to playback what you hear; you check your understanding and sometimes it helps them to clarify theirs. Paraphrasing aids memory and can instantly prevent misunderstanding.

'So what happened was…'
'You seem to be saying…'
'You're telling me that when you started here you thought you'd be a junior manager in five years and now six years on you don't see any sign of that.'

*Clarifying*
As well as seeking clarification from the speaker, this skill also underlines the message 'I really want to understand'. It is all too tempting to think you know what someone means or how they feel when the only indication they give is a vague 'you know' or an unfinished sentence. Clarifying enables you to focus on specific detail rather than generalisation.

'No I don't I don't think I do know what you mean...'
'I'm not sure whether it's the status, or having more
responsibility that is your major concern.'

*Encouragers*
These aim to keep the person talking with the minimum
input from you. One way is to repeat a word or short phrase
exactly as spoken by the other person. This encourages them
to say some more about that specific area. It often sounds
like a question.

'Junior manager?'
'You enjoy bargaining meetings.'

Another way of encouraging someone is to keep quiet and
nod your head or say 'aha', 'mm', 'yes' or 'OK'. The interviewee carries on talking confident that you are involved.

However, if you use encouragers too often you may find
you are not listening, just like a nodding dog.

*Silence*

Silence is helpful in two ways. First, it means you listen to the end of the sentence rather than butting in when you think you've understood enough. People sometimes need thinking time and the chance to breathe before carrying on. Second, it allows space between what you say and the other's response. It can take time to consider what you have said and how it affects them, especially if you have hit a sensitive area.

*Summarising*

This is a very useful skill for drawing together what has been said towards the end of a section of discussion or the end of the interview. A summary provides a final check for clarity after you have agreed certain actions or decisions and before you each go your separate ways.

> 'Let me see if this is right. You're feeling frustrated with your position in the company. You are worried that your work rate is falling dramatically and that seems guaranteed to block any hopes of movement. You're going to keep a record of what you are doing with your time over the next week and I'm going to look out training opportunities for you.'

## Questions

Once you have satisfied yourself and the interviewee that you have understood them, it is time to gather further information. Obviously the type of questioning you use will determine what you want to know or discuss next.

> *Types of question*
> - open questions
> - hypothetical questions
> - closed questions
> - keep off!

*Open questions*
Open questions do precisely that and open up an area of enquiry allowing the interviewee to expand on a subject in the way they choose.

> 'Could you tell me more about...?'
> 'What ideas do you have?'
> 'How might that affect your chances of promotion?'

Open questions usually start with the words how, what, which, when, where, who or why. Watch out when you are asking 'why' questions. Although they are open they can also seem interrogatory and abrasive.

*Hypothetical questions*
These questions encourage the speaker to use their imagination.

'What's your idea of our most difficult customer?'
'How would you handle them?'
'Where do you see yourself five years from now?'

Similar to brainstorming in training, you can work crazy
thoughts into innovative processes in one-to-one interviews.
Interviewees need to be clear that you genuinely want to
hear their ideas and are not trying to trap them. So avoid
using hypothetical questions in selection and recruitment
interviews. Candidates will try to give you the 'right'
answer.

*Closed questions*
Closed questions invite single word or yes/no answers.
They are useful when you want a precise piece of
information or when you want to stop someone from
waffling on. Use them sparingly; they can close the
discussion down before you are ready.

'Did you take responsibility for the accounts when
Sally was away?'
'Would you be interested in a sideways move?'

*Keep off!*
There are several forms of questioning which you should
avoid. Don't:

- Ask questions which relate to your interests or satisfy your curiosity.
  'This may not seem relevant but I've always been fascinated by your department's publicity...'
- Ask more than one question at a time.
  'Would you say your progress so far has been satisfactory? What sorts of promotions have you gone for? Are you thinking about moving on?'
  If you get an answer, to which of those will it relate?
- Answer your own question. 'How did you feel when Sue was promoted? Furious I expect.'
- Ask leading questions. 'You wouldn't want to upset anyone like that, would you?'

## Body language

It's not just what you say. The way that you say it makes a greater impact than the words themselves. All of the following can affect the outcome of an interview.

- **S**ound
- **H**abits
- **E**ye contact
- **P**osture

*Sound*
The way you use your voice in interviews can make all the difference to the message you convey. A genuine enquiry

into someone's workload can seem like a throwaway line (too quiet), an accusation (too loud), an apology (too rambling) or an unpleasant dig (sarcastic edge).

*Habits*

Have you ever been so distracted by someone clicking their pen or tapping their fingers that you lose the sense of what they are saying to you? Some of your gestures will be habitual responses whether you are fascinated, bored or pressurised by the interviewee. The problem is that you don't know what you are doing and the other person may misunderstand your intent. Ask your colleagues.

*Watch for*
- pointing finger or pen
- hands covering mouth
- inappropriate smile
- foot tapping

Do your gestures reinforce or contradict your message?

*Eye contact*
One way to show someone that you are interested in them
and what they are saying is to maintain steady eye contact
while they are talking. Just five to 10 seconds before looking
away is enough to demonstrate your attention. Over 10
seconds uninterrupted eye contact can start to become
intimidating. When your eyes wander, you may give an
impression of boredom, fear or insincerity. Notice how you
feel when different people look at you or away from you. If
you find eye contact difficult, look at the interviewee's
forehead or nose. That way you are concentrating on the
important area.

*Posture*
Consider how you sit when you are interviewing. If you
have your arms and legs crossed you will look unreceptive
and you are likely to be feeling tense. Open up and you can
breathe more freely and communicate accessibility. Lean
forward to give yourself more impact.

Think about the space between you and the interviewee.
Some people are comfortable sitting closely together while
others can feel claustrophobic. Be sensitive to comfort zones.

## Obstacles

On Sunday, we looked at organisational hindrances to an
effective interview. Below, we consider some *attitudes* which
can be hindrances to an effective interview.

*Comparing*

This is a hindrance because you are likely to be trying to
assess whether the interviewee is cleverer than you or more
likely to catch the MD's eye. While they are talking you may
be thinking:

'Could she do it as well as me?'
'That's a better idea than any of mine.'

*Open ears – closed mind*

Sometimes you decide rather quickly that you can predict
how the conversation will continue. This may be because
you have talked to the person before or, more dangerously,
because someone else has 'forewarned' you. You think that
there is no reason to concentrate any longer as you will not
hear anything new. You may also become selective and only
hear the bits that fit in with your preconceptions. The better
you think you know someone the more likely you are to
make assumptions in your interview. These are dangerous.
You find that you have been following different trains of
thought and it will take ages to return to the same track.

*Red rag*

Each of us can identify words or phrases that cause
immediate emotional reactions. Similar to a bull chasing a
red rag we cease listening in order to jump and pounce on
the offending statement. Once colleagues have spotted these
words they can use them to take you away from your
agenda for the interview.

OH, PARDON!

*Distractions*

These can be irrelevant thoughts and/or images that come
to the forefront of your mind. (Did you remember to send
out that memo? How are you going to sort out that
misunderstanding with accounts? What's for lunch?) You
have to practise putting them on hold or making a quick
note so as not to be distracted for too long.

*Language*

Choose your language carefully and adapt it to the
interviewee.

## Checklist

You probably already use many of today's skills. If there are some that need refreshing or adding to your repertoire, try them out and see what happens at the next interview you hold. Think about effective interviews you have experienced. What skills were used and what made them work?

*Interview skills to remember*

- Listen carefully and actively.
- Make sure the interviewee has the chance to say what they want.
- Keep checking and showing that you understand.
- Think about your use of questions.
- Remember SHEP (Sound, Habits, Eye contact, Posture).

# Selection and recruitment

Having considered some general skills and objectives, today we will look specifically at interviewing for selection and recruitment.

*Selection interviews*
- preparation
- the interview
- follow up

## Preparation

Preparation, as always, is a most important step in the interview process.

*Type of interview*
Most recruitment interviews are held between two people; the candidate and the employer/manager. In some cases a panel is convened with staff from different parts of the organisation or section that has a vacancy. Alternatively, candidates will have a number of sequential one-to-one interviews with several interested parties.

A panel will need to meet before the interviews to agree on a chairperson and the areas they each want cover. It is a good idea to stick to your specific area and not to ask other people's questions. Obviously it does not look favourable if the panel is competing or squabbling during the interview. The candidate will be summing up the company too.

One drawback of both panel and sequential interviews is that co-ordinating diaries for busy people can be very difficult.

Today we will concentrate on one-to-one interviews.

*Purpose*
To be able to conduct an effective selection interview you need to think about your reason for choosing this method of recruitment over any other, for example, personality tests or references.

*Gathering information* One reason for the interview is to check out the information received from the candidate. This can be in the form of a c.v., a letter of application or an application form. You are looking for discrepancies on the forms; gaps, or questions not completed. Once questioned at interview, they can lead to completely new and unexpected material.

*Matching process* You want to match the candidate as closely as you can to the job description and the person specification. You are also looking for someone who will fit into your particular organisation. A charming individual with tons of qualifications but no dress sense will not suit an upmarket design centre.

> *For each post:*
> - Are you looking for a certain 'type' of person?
> - Are you looking for a specific set of skills?
> - If both, then is either more important?

The interviewee also uses the interview to assess how you and the company match their needs and expectations.

*Compare personalities* The interview allows you to put together a fuller picture of the interviewees. People can be very hard to separate in terms of paper qualifications and attributes but are very different when seen 'live'. You can use the interview to compare candidates' performances under pressure. This may be key to the appointment.

*Interview plan*
This is crucial to the success of your interview. Having clarified your objectives you can now plan to meet them. You will feel more confident and relaxed if you have a clear and easy-to-follow format that is the same for all candidates. This also acts as a safeguard against you being lead away from your agenda.

*Interview plan*
- setting the scene
- timing
- your questions
- their questions

*Setting the scene* As you saw on Sunday, your organisational preparation for the interviews will make an immediate impression on the candidates. Just as you will make some 'instant' judgements about them so they will deduce certain things about you.

It is easier to guarantee *no interruptions* if you have a secretary, but even without one you can put a notice on the door, transfer phone calls or take the phone off the hook. If you normally share an office you either need to agree that it can be yours for as long as necessary or to arrange to occupy another office.

Some people like to go to a local hotel for guaranteed privacy, but that way they deny candidates the opportunity to look at their potential workplace and sample the atmosphere. They could think you have something to hide.

*Timing* Decide a schedule that allows you time to interview, reflect, write notes and prepare for the next person. Most interviews will take between 20 minutes and half an hour. You may need longer for second and panel interviews or when filling senior posts.

It is important to leave yourself a minimum of 10 minutes between each candidate. This gives you time to complete your notes and ideas on the previous applicant and prepare to concentrate on the next. If you plan to drink tea or coffee with candidates, leave yourself space for natural breaks.

If you are running late, then let the waiting candidates know personally or from a colleague/secretary, thus signalling that you respect the value of their time too.

*Your questions* Prepare some questions for each candidate before the interview. Depending on their answers, your supplementaries may well differ. It is important to be consistent with each person. Here are some suggestions:

*Opening:*
- How was your journey?
- Do you know this area at all?

*Main frame*
- Why did you choose to study… at school/college/university?
- Which aspects of your training/education did you enjoy? Not enjoy?
- What made you choose a career in this field?
- You have been working for your present employer for a short/long time. What makes you want to move now?
- How do you think your career to date equips you for this post?
- What strengths could you bring to this job?
- What weaknesses might hamper you?

A word of warning. When considering your questions, be familiar with current equal opportunities legislation and your company policy. This also applies to advertising the post and the job descriptions. Check this with the personnel department and senior managers.

During the interview you should make brief notes of key points. If you have chosen informal seating arrangements think about using a clip board or the end of a table to rest your notepad. Remember that you have allowed at least 10 minutes after the interview to compile detailed notes to assist your final decision.

*Their questions* The candidate may have covered these throughout the interview. It is still worth checking whether they have anything to ask or to add about themselves. Most interviewees will have prepared questions for the interview. The sorts of questions people ask give you an insight into their priorities, thoughts and attitudes.

Just as you wanted clarification from their written application, they may identify missing information in the data you supplied. Be ready for *job-related* questions like:

- How did the vacancy arise?
- What achievements are you looking for in the first six/twelve months?
- Can you give me a clear picture of what the job involves?

They may ask you to explain more about reporting lines and appraisal/job evaluation. If you are not the only person responsible for the vacant post the applicant will want to know who to report to. Be ready for *organisational* questions like:

- How will my work be monitored?
- Who will assess my work?
- What appraisal system does the company run?
- How many people will report directly to me?

If someone is planning to stay with your company they will be keen to find out about career opportunities. Even if they do not aspire to managerial posts they will want to know what is available to keep them up to date in their particular field of work. Be ready for *personal development* questions like:

- What kind of staff development and training programme do you have?
- How do you determine eligibility for further training?
- Are there opportunities for day-release studies?

HOW DID THE VACANCY ARISE?

## The interview

The interview will follow a sequence. An opening stage to settle the applicant and possibly yourself, the main frame, their questions, which have already been covered, and the conclusion.

*Interview stages*
- opening stage
- main frame
- any questions
- ending

*Opening stage*
At this point you want to outline the structure of the interview and generally put the applicant and yourself at ease. After a general welcome and pleasantries you may want to say something like:

*Openers*
- I would like to clarify some points in your written application.
- Then I would like discuss your education and employment history as they relate to this post.
- I will briefly tell you about the company.
- Finally I will be pleased to answer any of your questions that haven't been covered.

A logical and stated structure ensures that you both know where you are going. Though you will have some standard, prepared questions for each candidate, they are only guidelines which will become millstones if you do not allow yourself any flexibility.

*Main frame*
Is there anything you have highlighted from the written application that needs clarification? Data regarding your candidates will derive from application forms, c.v.s, letters, personality and numerical tests. You will have re-read these before the interview and highlighted particular areas of interest and concern.

A word of warning. Beware of making assumptions from the written material and then spending the interview trying to prove them right or wrong.

Next you will want to gain a clear picture of the person's educational and working background. You will have used the person specification and job description to help you plan your questions. Build on this information to relate skills and personality to the vacant post. Talk about the vacancy and probe for ideas or possible problem areas.

'Your last three job changes look like sideways moves, how would you see this one?'

*Ending*
It is your responsibility to signal and close the interview. You may want to summarise where you have reached and what, if any, is the next stage.

'I am interviewing a number of candidates for this post. All interviews will be completed today and I will be able to inform you of the decision by Tuesday next week.'

Check that their expenses have been covered, thank the applicant for their time, stand up and show them out.

## Follow up

Here you need to consider what you have told the candidate you will do after the interview, write and consider your notes and then action your decisions. If no one stands out then do not be tempted to appoint the best of a bad lot. You may have to repeat the whole process and spend some extra time and money now rather than saddling the company with second best and generating future problems. Calling a couple of people back for a second interview may be enough to iron out your concerns.

When making your decision, bear in mind the following key points.

*Candidate's suitability:*
- qualifications
- similarities in prior employment
- ability to do the job
- initiative
- fit with job description
- fit with person specification

The candidates will be expecting a decision by whatever time and manner you agreed to contact them. Make sure you or a representative honour this commitment. If you haven't already taken references this is the time to do so, and any job offer will be subject to these being satisfactory.

## Checklist

There is plenty to think about in selection and recruitment interviews. By preparing fully and deciding your main objectives you can put all your energy into making the interview highly effective.

*Checklist questions*
- Are you clear about the job description and person specification?
- Have you checked what are facts and what are assumptions?
- How will you set out the interview room?
- Have you decided and listed your key questions?
- What might the interviewee ask you?
- Is there sufficient breathing space between interviews?

# Appraisal

On Tuesday, you interviewed and selected the best person
for the job. Today, we will consider one way of encouraging
them to stay with the organisation; appraisal. You promote a
two-way process of communication by conducting appraisal
interviews, which usually occur annually. Both parties need
to understand and appreciate that this is an opportunity to
exchange ideas, not an excuse for an annual slanging match.

*Appraisal interviews*
- the purpose
- preparation
- the interview
- follow up

## The purpose

Be clear about your company's definition and purpose of appraisal interviewing before you embark on any (or any more) staff appraisals. At the very least, an appraisal interview is a regular means of letting employees know how well they are performing in relation to established standards. It also provides the opportunity for them to air their views about their employment.

*Possible purposes of appraisal*

Organisational
- reduce staff turnover
- identify employees' strengths and weaknesses
- provide data for manpower planning
- improve in-company communication

Managerial
- improve present performance
- assess development or promotion potential
- set objectives for performance
- discover appraisee's ambitions
- obtain information for pay review

Individual
- recognition for jobs well done
- review performance
- discuss weaknesses and how to improve
- gain commitment for training
- chart possible career progression

Does the company have policy documents setting out their expectations? Is there an appraisal handbook?

You also need to consider who in the company will have access to the content of the interview and whether this is recorded or reported. The appraisee needs to know this too. It will affect what they say during the interview.

*Performance and pay*
Wherever possible it is a good idea to separate a performance appraisal from a pay review. You want to encourage open and frank discussion with the appraisee. This is much more difficult when they believe that they must show only their successes to be sure of the best pay award. Equally you may find yourself having to grade the appraisee to fit the monetary amounts available for rewarding good performance. This can lead to you pre-judging a series of interviews to fit your finances. Another advantage of separating the two functions is that following the appraisal, your employee can work on any agreed improvements before the pay review takes place.

## Preparation

Preparation is crucial for the appraisal interview. It is essential that both you and your appraisee have at least ten days' notice of the meeting. This gives you both time to consider fully your own agendas.

You will have to set aside time to read last year's appraisal and think about the one in hand. In fact you must make time to read all the relevant paperwork before structuring your interview. If your company uses a prepared form this will give you an outline of what you should be working towards.

*Useful documentation*
- previous appraisals
- job description
- performance standards
- notes from the year's events
- employee records
- reports from others
- training data
- examples to support feedback
- blank appraisal form
- appraisee's self-assessment
- appraisee's agenda

Many companies also provide appraisees with a form on which they can make notes and consider their approach to the interview. The appraisee can return this to you before the interview if they wish. If you both have time you can arrange a short meeting to discuss agenda items so that at the appraisal you both know what to expect and don't need to spend time negotiating.

### No surprises

An appraisal is not a time for surprises. You will be discussing issues that have arisen throughout the year and including positives as well as areas for improvement. With appraisal in mind, you may have made notes since the last formal meeting of what you both said and did on significant occasions. You will need to refer to these before the interview.

### Reports from others

If you are the appraisee's main manager, who else has relevant information about their work? You will need to talk to them before the interview. This can be time consuming, especially if there are any personality clashes. It is important here to collect facts and evidence regarding the appraisee's work behaviour rather than hearsay or unsubstantiated opinions. You may have to balance and make judgements about quite differing pictures of the same person.

*Timing*

You should both allow an hour and a half for the interview. This gives you some time after the appraisal to collect your thoughts and make any notes before returning to everyday work. If the interview runs for longer than an hour it is worth thinking about arranging a follow up rather than slogging on to the bitter end. You will both be tired and cease to be effective.

As we saw on Monday, active listening involves a great deal of concentration. You may be surprised at how much energy you use. Remember this when you consider how many appraisals you would be able to handle in any one day. If you have more than a couple of staff to appraise it would be a good idea to spread out your interviews over the year.

## The interview

It is important to create a balanced interview. As well as recognising and praising the interviewee's strengths, be clear about the areas for improvement. The interviewee should leave feeling positively challenged.

*Purpose*

A good way to start the appraisal interview is to remind the appraisee why you are both there. It is likely that they are feeling apprehensive and uncertain, especially if this is their first appraisal with you or your company. This is an interview that is recorded and can affect their promotion and pay prospects. You have already clarified the purpose for yourself; now let them know. Emphasise that this is an opportunity for constructive dialogue and discussion. Let them know if you plan to make brief notes and suggest they can take some too.

*Agenda*

This may have already been arranged at a short meeting before the appraisal interview. You will both have topics that you want to cover and most will probably overlap. At this point you need to outline the order you want to take and agree it.

*Do you start with:*
- the appraisee's weaknesses?
- their strengths?
- appraisee's assessment of the above?

*Do you follow:*
- the appraisal form in strict order?
- the job description statement by statement?

*When to mention:*
- training?
- next year's targets?

Whichever you decide, let the appraisee know. Keep an open mind and if the discussion goes out of sequence for a good reason, follow the flow.

Remember active listening from Monday. Make sure you give them ample opportunity to convey their thoughts and ideas. Don't dominate.

*Key areas to cover*
- last year's appraisal and targets
- problems over the year
- successes over the year
- areas for improvement/training/development
- performance standards past/future
- areas of job dis/satisfaction
- agreed future targets

## Giving feedback

The most effective way to give and receive feedback is in an atmosphere of safety and trust. Remember, appraisal is a two-way process; if you have criticisms of an employee's work be aware that they might also want to criticise you.

> *Giving feedback*
> - be specific
> - behaviour/effects on others
> - feelings
> - their ideas/possible changes
> - outcomes

*Be specific*
Whether your feedback is positive or negative, it is best to refer to specific incidents you have observed or been told about. You want to encourage development and self-awareness in your appraisee. You will not do so by saying, 'that was great' or 'you were lousy'. Give clear examples.

> 'I'd like to discuss your role on the safety committee. I am aware that the minutes are still taking over two weeks to be circulated'.
> 'Let's look at the last time the representative from Hollands was here...'

*Behaviour/effect on others*
Before offering a criticism think about what part of their behaviour it is that you want to comment on. You either want someone to change for improvement or to continue with behaviour that is effective. You may also have something to say about the effect these behaviours have on others.

If you are suggesting change, then you need to be sure that it is something the appraisee is able to change. Comments like, 'if you'd had experience of an office fire you'd understand the urgency' are most unhelpful. Better to say something like:

> 'Decisions taken at the health and safety committee affect all staff. When you delay writing up the minutes colleagues become anxious.'

Be clear when you are reinforcing the positives.

> '...I was pleased to see you listening to her, letting her finish what she was saying and then summarising your agreed plan of action. She looked pleased too.'

## Feelings

It is important to express how you feel about the situation. This can be a way of letting the appraisee know the strength of your criticism or praise.

> 'I was pleased...' '...and I'm delighted.'
> 'I feel increasingly annoyed when...' '...I was left feeling extremely uncomfortable.'

## Their ideas/possible changes

These are key to the appraisal process. Your aim is to reach an agreement that is acceptable to both of you; this will be

more successful than imposing your own ideas without
discussion. Very often if you ask for an appraisee's ideas or
suggestions for change, they will have plenty to say. After
all, they will know about these matters as they have been
dealing with them throughout the year. If you don't elicit
their ideas you will lose their commitment.

*Outcomes*
What are the possible consequences of the behaviour you
are discussing? These can have a bearing on whether you
reach an agreement about the need for change.

> 'It is vital that the minutes are circulated within 48
> hours. If this doesn't happen we will appear
> disinterested in safety issues.'
>
> 'If you continue to practise active listening you'll find
> negotiating much easier.'

## Receiving feedback

During the appraisal interview you will be asking for
comments from your appraisee and seeking ideas for
change. It is quite possible that some of these may include
criticisms directed at you. **Listen** to what the appraisee is
saying, and consider it carefully before responding. There
may be something for you to learn too.

*Receiving criticism*

Don't
- deny the criticism
- become defensive
- argue
- sulk
- justify yourself

Do
- listen carefully
- ask for clarification
- decide whether the comment is valid
- if true – what can be done?
- if not/partly true – how has this impression come about?
- agree change
- what have you learned?

## Action plan and summary

Aim to have clear agreements of targets and actions for the following twelve months. The action plan should include review dates and success criteria. Agree any training opportunities you've discussed and their implementation.

Your summary will consist of a recap of any jointly agreed problems, agreed changes, development plans and areas of satisfaction. You can indicate what you will be including in the written appraisal document, and when you will be handing it to the appraisee for their comments and signature.

Whenever possible, aim to end the interview on a positive note even if you seem to be asking for a great many changes rather than encouraging them to keep up the good work. Remind them about the areas you are pleased with and emphasise that you have reached joint agreements in the areas for improvement. This is vital to ensure their commitment.

## Follow up

Most companies require a formal record of the appraisal interview. Whether this is on a pre-designed form or left for you to organise, write it as soon as you can after the interview. During the interview you will have taken brief notes of the most important points. This is the time to expand on them in greater detail.

Put into operation any agreements you reach with your appraisee. These could include organising training, taking up coaching opportunities or arranging counselling. As soon

as this process is completed you can start collecting
information for next year's appraisal.

## Checklist

Most people want to know how they are getting on at work.
Even though you are talking to them throughout the year,
the appraisal interview offers the chance to consider past
and future projects in detail. The added bonus is that they
have your complete attention.

*Checklist questions*
- Will the interview be in your office, their office or a
  neutral meeting place?
- Have you agreed the date and time in advance?
- Have you collected and read all the relevant
  documentation?
- What is your agenda? How does it compare with
  theirs?
- What are the key areas for feedback – positives and
  areas for improvement?
- When will you summarise agreed actions?
- Can you deliver your promises and they theirs?

# Coaching

Coaching is an ongoing part of a manager's workload which, over time, will help you increase the motivation and effectiveness of your staff. The coaching process is likely to involve at least two interviews with a clear action element sandwiched in between. Unlike appraisal, which usually occurs annually, coaching interviews occur throughout the working year. They don't have to be formal, and indeed can be very successful when spontaneous.

Telling team members that a job has been well done is an integral part of the coaching process. Most people need to feel wanted and coaching is a way of giving employees a confidence boost and faith in themselves.

*Coaching interviews*
- purpose
- preparation
- opening interview
- follow up – review interview

Coaching is not to be confused with training. Training off the job involves going away to a classroom environment or working on distance learning packages before returning to implement the learning at work. On-the-job training involves 'sitting with Nellie' when someone is new to a task or organisation. They first watch a colleague perform the operation before being observed as they take it on. The key to coaching is that, after you have identified and agreed a learning opportunity, you leave the individual to perform the task alone. The role of the manager is to debrief thoroughly the staff member **before** and **after** the event.

You therefore have several options available to you, which are summarised below. You need to decide which is the best one; best for you, the manager, best for the organisation and best for the interviewee. All have a place in closing the gap between the standard required and present performance.

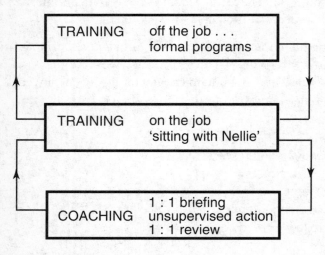

Adapted from Rapport CC

## Purpose

Coaching interviews enable individual development in two distinct ways. Many companies only use coaching when mistakes are being made or when someone fails to reach the required standards. Its other application is to recognise potential and then empower employees to acknowledge their strengths and understand their accomplishments.

Coaching involves
- improving poor performance
- building on competence and success

*Improving poor performance*
When someone is clearly not reaching the agreed standards at work or is consistently repeating an error, they tend to be sent for training, and if that doesn't work, they are often disciplined. Coaching provides an interim measure for achieving the desired improvement. By spending time with the individual, you can work through the difficulties and agree a plan of action for them to follow. Then it is vital to arrange a review interview and assess what has happened. This is different from disciplining an employee because the underlying objective is that of looking for learning indicators from the experience.

For example:

Chris is increasingly avoiding a particular customer whose account is her responsibility. A first coaching interview will explore why, involve her ideas in encouraging her to make contact and then let her do it. At the second interview you can review what happened. This is better than just telling her to get out there and do her job.

*Building on competence and success*
This is where coaching comes into its own. By developing
your staff and increasing their confidence you will also be
developing the organisation and creating space for your
own growth. You will be able to delegate more and so leave
space to extend your competencies. Take great care to check
that you are delegating meaningful tasks, not just dumping
the ones you don't like.

*Coaching increases*
- employees' confidence and risk taking
- employees' autonomy
- employees' skills and abilities
- a sense of partnership between manager and
  employee
- job satisfaction

It may be that you want to prepare an employee to take over when you are on leave, at a training course or need them to chair a meeting in your absence. You may assign someone to run a specific project or second them to another department. Each time you use such incidents as coaching opportunities you will be enabling your staff to learn and understand their learning. By spending time with them in the short term you will save time in the long term as their confidence to make decisions increases.

## Preparation

*Preparation*
- identify opportunities
- consider learning styles
- clarify objectives
- documentation

*Identify opportunities*
If the organisation is planning changes in procedure or staffing that will directly affect you and your team, then this will predetermine your coaching opportunities. In other instances, it is your responsibility to know your team's abilities and be looking for development. It may be that someone is expressing boredom or is clearly on top of all their responsibilities; this may be a case of preparing for promotion however far away that may be. Finally you may have to act if someone is regularly making errors or not

performing satisfactorily. In each case, there is a gap in
performance or motivation that can be filled through
coaching.

*Consider learning styles*
Before you enter into a coaching interview, think about the
way your interviewee likes, and is open to, learning.
Learners can be broadly classified into four styles, and it is
important to match the coaching interview to your
interviewee's preferred style. You will need to consider this
beforehand to make most effective use of the interview.

### Learning types

- **activist**    likes to learn by getting involved in
  projects straight away. Doesn't like to
  sit and watch.
- **reflector**   likes time to prepare and consider
  before action. Observes first and then
  performs.
- **theorist**    likes to see systems, theories and
  models. Fits facts into theories for
  understanding.
- **pragmatist**  likes to put practical application into
  ideas. Concentrates on job-related
  issues.

Many people favour just one of the styles while some can
adapt to two or three. If you can be alert to this before the
opening interview it is more likely to be successful. Just as

activists do not like to sit through repetitious practice sessions, reflectors will not perform well if they are thrown in at the deep end without warning.

Consider your own learning style. It may be quite different from your interviewee's, and this could affect your understanding in the coaching interview. Part of your preparation for the opening interview could well involve consciously putting aside how you would tackle things and being ready to listen to their approach.

*Clarify objectives*
Be clear about why you have taken this coaching opportunity. Consider how it will have an impact on the organisation as well as the interviewee and yourself. Whilst you may be used to setting work goals with your staff, in the coaching interview you will be setting learning goals too. So that for Chris who was avoiding contacting a customer (Green), the work goal would be regular contact with Green. The learning goal would be understanding and eliminating the anxieties that prevented it.

Take time to check that the goals you are aiming at are clear
in your mind. They may change during the interview but
you need to start with a specific task that is measurable and
achievable whilst stretching for the interviewee.

*Documentation*

- Are there any papers or forms that the interviewee
  will need to assist them with their task?
- Are there personal contacts they will need to make?
- What ideas/experience do you have to offer?
- Are there any legal requirements?

Always remembering that this is a chance for the
interviewee to establish their own learning, you can still
have ideas and suggestions available if required.

## Opening interview

The opening interview is the first bite of the coaching
sandwich. This where you discuss the task to be undertaken,
elicit the interviewee's ideas and help them consider any
concerns. Whereas on Wednesday, in the appraisal
interview, you were surveying the interviewee's whole year,
here you are working through one activity at a time.

*Scene setting*
This interview need not necessarily take place in your office.
Depending on the layout of your workplace, it may be as
easy to go to the interviewee's work station or office for the

discussion. You will want to ensure that wherever you choose is comfortable for both of you, is conducive to good listening, and is sufficiently private to avoid others' attention. It is a good idea to pick a time when you both can spare at least twenty minutes to guarantee a full dialogue. The ideal is a relaxed atmosphere and a shared knowledge that this is an important interview.

*Encourage and enable*

The coaching interview is definitely not a tell-sell interview. Your aim is to encourage the interviewee to work out their own goals and the methods they choose to achieve them. There will of course be an element of control from you in the sense that you may initially influence the area to be worked on. You will also need to clarify the limits of their responsibility. What authority do they have, and what level of decisions can they make without referring to you?

As a manager you are used to devising and giving out instructions; as a coach the emphasis changes to one of listening and support. This may seem strange at first and it is worth considering what can help or hinder that process.

*Helping strategies*

- Give the interviewee time to think through the issues. After all you have prepared for this interview; they might not have thought about it before.
- Accept when the interviewee has doubts about their ability. Rather than the all too common, 'I know you can do it', acknowledge their concern and investigate it together, 'tell me what's bothering you'.
- Encourage the interviewee to put forward their own ideas and suggestions.
- Respect those ideas and listen with an open mind.
- Although not expecting mistakes, be clear they will be accepted as learning opportunities, not something to be feared.
- Ensure that any special projects are seen to be worthwhile and useful to the organisation not just an excuse for keeping the interviewee occupied.
- Be clear that you will stand back and let the interviewee perform the agreed actions.

*Unhelpful strategies*

- Avoid dependency caused by imposing solutions or being too quick to put your views forward.
- Don't dump routine tasks or ones you don't like.
- Take care not to become involved in or to provoke an argument.
- Refrain from smothering the interviewee's attempts at showing initiative.
- Don't try to be too clever or use the interview to score points against the interviewee.

*Key questions*

> *Questions checklist*
> - elicit opinions on the task
>   What do you think about…?
>   Have you considered…?
>   I've noticed… How do you see it?
>   What experiences have you had so far?
> - discuss possible actions
>   How might you tackle it?
>   Who else do you need to involve?…. When?
>   What would you do first?… Second?
>   What is your timescale?
> - consider pitfalls
>   What problems do you envisage?
>   Have you thought about…?
>   Are there any obstacles that spring to mind?

In the main you will be concentrating on using the open questions we described on Monday. Your aim is to assist the interviewee to work out their action plan and timetable as they see it. Part of your role in the interview is to check that they consider the subject from as many angles as possible. You want to encourage them to set themselves up for success not failure. Only put forward your own suggestions when you are sure the interviewee has exhausted theirs. And remember they are only suggestions.

*Agree action*
Make sure that you are both clear and in agreement about the action to be taken.

'Chris you are going to phone Green on Wednesday afternoon and make an appointment to go through the account in person at a meeting to be arranged. You would like to visit their offices and see the system in operation. We have agreed tactics to cover the sarcasm you received before and you are happy, if a little bit nervous, to implement them if necessary. We will meet on Wednesday week to discuss the outcomes.'

If required, part of the coaching role may be to rehearse a situation during the opening interview. This way you can observe the interviewee's current way of dealing with things, understand their concerns and increase their confidence.

*Wait and see*

This can be the hardest part of the coaching process. You are taking a risk when increasing someone's responsibilities, knowing that ultimately the buck stops at your door. If you have briefed them fully in the opening interview you are most likely to be pleased with the outcome.

An added risk is that there is a chance they will perform better than you and may become a threat to your own position. This can explain the fear some managers have of delegation; that increasing another's expertise can endanger your prospects. This depends on the culture of the organisation you work for. Where coaching is encouraged, then everyone is working towards greater autonomy in a supportive environment, not just your staff. In an authoritarian culture you are unlikely to make much progress.

## Follow up – review interview

This is an integral part of the coaching process, which you should not neglect. You will have arranged a date at the opening interview. This is your opportunity to assess together the learning and experience gained from the activity.

> *Review interview*
> - self-assessment
> - feedback
> - what next?

*Self-assessment*
Resist the temptation to overwhelm the interviewee with a list of strengths and weaknesses which you have observed or imagined may have occurred. Another coaching opportunity is to assist the interviewee to develop self-critical skills in areas of strength and weakness. Many of us are quick to identify failings and errors but tend to dismiss our successes. It is up to you to help the interviewee take a reasoned approach to both. You may want them to consider:

- What went well?
- What pleased you?
- What could you have done differently?
- Which were the problem points?
- What facilitated you?
- What held you back?

You are asking questions to help the interviewee think through the issue and make their own decisions. Don't impose your own solutions and values.

*Feedback*
When you are both satisfied that you have covered the interviewee's assessment it is appropriate to give your own feedback. It may be worth spending a few minutes outlining your understanding of feedback and its purpose so as to avoid defensiveness or inertia. As we saw on Wednesday in the appraisal interview, this can be exceedingly helpful if given in a supportive and positive way. Your aim is to consolidate and confirm the new knowledge and skills gained by the interviewee and to reinforce what they have done well.

Help them to understand any mistakes and enable them to learn new strategies.

*What next?*
There is no guaranteed outcome to a coaching interview. Much depends on the nature of the initial tasks. If everything has gone well you may both want to consider further challenges for the interviewee on an agreed structural basis. If the review interview throws up a basic operational problem it may be that the interviewee needs to go for more or first time off-the-job training. If they are nearly there, but still lacking the confidence to act alone, you may want to send them back to 'Nellie' for a while. Whichever option you finally agree, be careful that you have approached it with an open mind after a thorough review.

## Checklist

The coaching interview enables you and the interviewee to develop their existing skills in many different ways. You may be preparing them to deputise for you in the case of holidays, or letting them take more responsibility in one particular section of work. The more you coach effectively, the greater your capacity for self-improvement too.

> *Remember*
> - Be on the lookout for coaching opportunities.
> - Consider the interviewee's learning style especially if it differs from yours.
> - Listen to their ideas and suggestions before offering yours.
> - Wait and see – don't interfere unnecessarily.
> - Help them analyse their experiences – don't do it for them.

# Counselling

The counselling interview differs from those on the other days because it can be initiated by your employee rather than yourself. It is possible that you may notice a change in someone's behaviour, attitude or appearance that leads you to invite them to talk to you. Be sure to **invite** them to talk to you and not compel them. If you try to force them to disclose all you will only alienate them.

*Counselling interviews*
- general preparation
- the interview
- follow up

A counselling interview is not a disciplinary interview. Your role is much more one of helper than manager. You are there to assist the interviewee come to terms with whatever is worrying them through understanding and acceptance.

## General preparation

It is important to consider how you might handle a
counselling interview. There is a good chance that you
won't be able to prepare for each specific case, and no two
cases are the same because of the individuality of those
involved. If you have thought about the following
guidelines they will stand you in good stead. You are not
expected to be a professional counsellor by the end of today,
just someone more comfortable with issues of a personal
nature.

*General preparation*
- relationship
- confidentiality
- timing
- location

*The relationship*
This is one instance where you have to quell your
managerial instinct to tell someone what to do or find the
solution to their problems. You have to remember that what
they describe is their problem, not yours. Resist the
temptation to take over the problem. This is one time when
it is not appropriate to say, 'Leave it with me and I'll sort it
out.' In a counselling relationship you are initially providing
a safe and private place for someone to discuss and think
about issues that are affecting them at work, at home or
both. You are not there as an expert or adviser, but as a
concerned individual wanting to help them handle a
difficulty or make a decision.

*In the counselling relationship you*
- don't need specialist knowledge
- don't have to have all the answers
- don't take over the other's problems
- don't do it for them

Central to the counselling relationship are three key attitudes that you will need to convey to your interviewee. Known as REG, they help to ensure a beneficial interview.

*Key attitudes*
**R**espect is:
- openness and acceptance of the interviewee
- suspending judgement and criticism
- considering they are worth listening to

**E**mpathy is:
- understanding the interviewee's viewpoint
- putting yourself in their shoes
- understanding how they feel

**G**enuineness is:
- a sincere interest in the interviewee
- being consistent and straightforward

It takes courage to talk to a manager at work about personal issues, all the more so if the employee thinks they will be laughed at or belittled. REG enables you to concentrate on understanding, not judging.

*Confidentiality*

This may well depend on the types of issues you are discussing. In most cases you will be discussing issues outside work, and will need to agree that the matters discussed go no further. If other staff are involved you have to decide between the two of you whether to include those people in the conversation. Matters relating to health and safety might mean talking to a higher authority, and both you and the employee needs to be clear about what is going to happen. Once someone has felt able to confide in you and been accepted, it is likely that they will know and agree if someone else needs to be brought in.

Take care not to breach confidentiality by treating the interviewee differently after a counselling interview because of your 'inside information'. Resist the temptation to make excuses for their behaviour or to cover up for them. Comments like, 'If you knew what a time he's having with his teenager…' are a betrayal of confidence. You only need to break one confidence to become known as unreliable and untrustworthy.

*Timing*

If you have arranged the interview beforehand you can
ensure that you leave yourself at least thirty minutes, no
more than an hour, for the session. Add ten minutes to
reflect and initiate any agreed actions. Any longer than an
hour will probably mean that you start to go over old
ground. It is better to arrange a second interview than keep
going until you both collapse. If you are approached
without warning you may not be able to put things on hold
straight away. The minimum you should aim at is a few
minutes to get an idea of the subject matter, and then an
agreement to meet later at a mutually acceptable time.
People can hold on to their concerns if they know you are
interested and will be available when you say. If you try to
tackle a counselling interview when you are busy thinking
about your own work schedule, REG won't be with you and
neither will you be with the employee.

*Location*

More than ever this needs to be somewhere quiet and free
from interruptions. If you work in a very busy office where
people can see, if not hear, what you are doing, then you
will have to take over someone else's office. You may have
to go for a walk outside the building. It is not a good idea to
go to a pub or social club as you can confuse roles and are in
greater danger of breaching confidence. The counselling
interview will only be successful in a private, unhurried and
confidential setting. It is your responsibility to provide it.

## The interview

The counselling interview can be divided into three stages.
This is not a rigid structure and you will often move around
the stages. Some interviewees will only need you for the
first, listening stage; others may go to the second, while
some may need all three.

Throughout the counselling interview you will need to use
the skills of active listening as described on Monday.

*Three stages of the counselling interview*

Stage 1 Understanding
- What is the interviewee's story?
- How do they feel?
- Is there more than one concern?

Stage 2 Moving on
- Is there another way of looking at things?
- How have others managed?
- How many options are there?

Stage 3 Action
- Goal setting
- Provide ongoing support
- Review and evaluation

*Stage 1 Understanding*
At the beginning of a counselling interview give your full
attention to understanding what the problem or issue really

is. People often worry about things for ages before deciding to take the risk and talk about them, or before their behaviour means they are called to account. Once they start talking you may have to sort out a jumble of emotions and ideas.

Your first task is hold back and **listen** with undivided attention. You can expect to do about 70% listening at this stage and only 30% talking. This enables them to clarify their concerns. Don't write notes – the interviewee will be wary of what you might use the information for. Use open questions, paraphrasing, clarifying and encouraging responses to enable the interviewee to start unpacking their story.

One aim of an effective counselling interview is to help the interviewee recognise and accept their feelings. Feelings are important and if they are not expressed they can restrict a person's ability to make decisions or choices. Most people are happier talking about their thoughts and they might need you to help them find the 'feeling' words.

Compare: 'I feel I would work better if there was some chance of promotion', with: 'I feel frustrated and stuck with career possibilities here'.

The first statement describes how the person is thinking about their performance, the second tells how they feel and is much more personally revealing. The opportunity to express feelings in a safe setting enables them to be released and to lessen the anxiety so that the interviewee is able to think and eventually act more constructively.

It is very important in this stage to accept the interviewee's viewpoint and their feelings even if they are not the same as yours. If you start telling them how you would deal with things, they lose an opportunity to develop their own coping mechanisms. They may even feel further undermined if your solution is a simple one.

Resist the temptation to rush through Stage 1 at the cost of not fully exploring all the issues. The interviewee may start by talking about a safe subject before feeling able to talk about the more difficult concern.

Once you are clear about the problem you can move on to Stage 2 if they want to. Just talking may have been enough. Some situations don't have a solution or easy answer. The skill then in Stage 1 is to allow your interviewee time to air them. People will often thank you for just listening attentively when everyone else is full of ideas and answers.

*Stage 2 Moving on*
In this stage of the counselling interview you will be helping the interviewee to see if there are other ways of considering

their dilemma. People sometimes get stuck in a particular thought pattern and believe there is only one way of looking at their situation. You can help the interviewee to explore alternatives and look for options. Even though you may be doing a little more of the talking in this stage of the interview you still need REG to be with you.

*Stage 2 skills*
- Feedback
  'Perhaps people find it hard to take you seriously because you always laugh and play down your achievements.'
- Probing
  'What would happen if you did that?'
- Challenging
  'You said you wanted to work with someone else, and when we arranged the office move you didn't want to go. Where does that leave us?'
- Sharing your own experience
  'I remember feeling very anxious the first time I had to speak to the directors. It gets easier.'

*Be warned this is not an excuse to start telling the interviewee about your problems. It is not a competition.*

You need to have developed a trusting relationship to be able to challenge the interviewee in this stage of the interview. You are not trying to catch them out and show them up. They may be aware of the point you are making and still find it hard to accept. Give them time to think things through, avoid too much too quickly. Challenge carefully and with caring.

At the end of Stage 2 you will have considered alternative ways of looking at the situation and various opportunities.

*Stage 3 Action*
Once the interviewee has considered all the options available to them they may feel confident to go away and do whatever they see fit. However, they may still want you to help them put together an action plan. This involves helping them set realistic goals and not imposing your own solutions. As a manager you are often expected to know what's best and see that it happens. In the counselling interview your job is to help the interviewee come to their own conclusions. You need to help them work towards **manageable** targets. If their goal is enormous, like eating an elephant, the best way is to take one bite at a time.

*Stage 3 skills*

- Goal setting
  Make sure the interviewee's goal is clear, specific
  and is attainable.
- Resourcing
  You may be able to alter shifts, extend leave,
  arrange a transfer.
- Reviewing
  Offer ongoing support to check progress, evaluate
  and possibly change goals over time.
- Referral
  Don't work outside your competence or comfort
  level. Know when to stop and use outside agencies.
  The address below may be useful if you need to
  refer to an outside agency:

British Association for Counselling
1 Regent Place
Rugby
CV21 2PJ

01788 578328

Whatever help you offer in Stage 3, be sure to limit it to
what the interviewee cannot do for themselves. Again resist
the temptation to take over and 'get it sorted'.

Your contribution at this stage may include helping with a
thorough examination of what may help or hinder the
interviewee's chosen goal.

- Are there people who will aid or encourage the interviewee? (Friends, colleagues, family.)
- Are there situations that help or hinder? (Working alone, with others, in a noisy atmosphere.)

It is important to think these through and be prepared for any pitfalls.

## Follow up

Unlike any of the other interviews that you conduct there is no organised follow up after the counselling interview. You will obviously go ahead and take any actions you agreed on the interviewee's behalf. You now need to act as though nothing has happened and put the interviewee's personal issues to one side. Destroy any notes you may have made or give them back to the interviewee.

You may want to arrange another discussion for a later date to check progress. This way the interviewee knows you are still interested in them and it wasn't a one-off interview.

Continue watching for signs of personal problems that may be affecting your staff's performances and behaviour. Once they know you are approachable you can deal with many issues before they are blown up out of proportion and are much harder to manage.

## Checklist

Counselling interviews are less likely to be planned than
any of the other interviews. You have to expect the
unexpected and be ready. You are not 'in-charge' of the
interviewee but are more of a sounding board. Giving time
to your interviewee when they need it can save time and
crises later on.

*A counselling checklist*
- Remember REG (**R**espect, **E**mpathy, **G**enuineness).
- Give plenty of time to listening especially in Stage 1
  – understanding
- Help the interviewee express their feelings.
- Notice who is doing most of the talking.
- Don't jump into problem-solving.
- You're not expected to have all the answers; there
  may not be any.
- Be clear about confidentiality.

# Discipline

Many managers and supervisors are apprehensive about discipline. They let small incidents go unchecked rather than tackling situations as they arise. The result may be loss of respect from staff and difficulties with senior managers when the situation eventually has to be handled.

*Disciplinary interviews*
- company policy
- preparation
- the interview
- dos and don'ts.

## Company policy

The company is likely to have a discipline code or set of rules that are available to all staff. These cover such areas as: timekeeping, absence, Health and Safety and the use of company property and facilities, as well as detailing those offences that constitute gross misconduct. You need to be familiar with them and know how far your responsibility goes. Are you only expected to carry out the first informal interview or do you have the authority to go right to the end culminating in dismissal?

There should also be established procedures for discipline, though sometimes these only relate to formal disciplinary interviews. If you don't adhere to the procedures set out you could damage your case if it were to go to a tribunal. Where there is no existing procedure, check with colleagues for guidance and to see what has happened before. It is also important to find out the various stages of discipline that your company follows. You may want to contact ACAS (the Advisory Conciliation and Arbitration Service) whose code of practice sets out useful and well-tested ground rules.

ACAS
London Region
Clifton House
83–117 Euston Road
NW1 2RB

0171 396 0022

## Preparation

Preparation is crucial for the disciplinary interview. It is vital that as many facts as possible are collected whatever the level of formality.

*Purpose*

Why are you holding this interview? In the case of the
formal disciplinary interview it may be the last in a line of
procedures which lead to terminating the interviewee's
employment. Less formal interviews often represent an
attempt to improve performance or standards so that the
interviewee accepts the need for change and remains with
the company. In some cases, the interviewee may be
hampered by matters beyond their control and if so, you
need to know about it. Then the disciplinary interview
serves to eliminate the problem, not just to castigate the
interviewee. Generally your aim will be to detect the
situation before it leads to dismissal.

*Information*

Whatever the stage of discipline you will need to have
collected as much information as possible.

### Information gathering
- Records – timekeeping, attendance, sales,
  performance statistics.
- Paperwork – previous interviews, reports from other
  managers, warning letters.
- People – witnesses, other employees, customers'
  complaints,  suppliers' complaints (written
  allegations from complainant).

You would not expect to gain information from all these
sources each time. Whatever you do collect, make sure it is

relevant and dated, and itemise it in note form for the interview.

In some instances, you will not have hard evidence to support a complaint. However, it is still important to continue with the interview and give the interviewee a chance to put over their assessment of the situation.

A full investigation will take some time to organise. If there is any health, safety or security risk to the company or employees (fighting, drunk in charge of machinery, etc.) those concerned should be suspended on full pay until the disciplinary interview.

*Notes*
Make clear and specific notes for each item you wish to cover. You should indicate the positive aspects of the interviewee's work as well when it is appropriate. Be clear that if only one section of an otherwise effective workload is causing difficulties that this is presented in context.

---

*Alec*
- response to phonecalls: complaints from other depts. of bored, offhand approach, hope Alec won't answer
- very skilled researcher, concise written reports, delivers data to time
- ? problems with telephone technique?
  ? responding to others interferes with 'his work'?

---

Have all your points listed so that you can go through and check them off as you conduct the interview.

*Notice*

You may choose a quick informal interview there and then if you happen to be on site as an incident occurs. Otherwise you will need to give the interviewee notice that you want to speak with them. They need time to prepare themselves and any presentation they wish to make. Depending on the formality of the forthcoming interview, you may both wish to have observers who will also need notice of the meeting.

*Timing*

Consider how you think the interviewee will respond in the interview. If they are likely to be very upset or angry, it may be wise to set the interview at the end of a day, a shift or even a week. That way they can go home without having to face colleagues, customers or machinery.

## The interview

There are a number of points along the disciplinary continuum where it is appropriate to hold an interview. Whether you are engaged at the very informal or most formal stage of the process you must endeavour to hold the interview in private. You are not aiming to humiliate the interviewee in front of customers or workmates; there is a chance that they will join in too. This could prejudice the outcome of the interview.

- type of interview
- procedure
- notes

*Type of interview*

The type of interview you are likely to hold will depend on the circumstances and seriousness of each case. You need to be clear with yourself and the employee at which stage of the disciplinary procedure you are operating.

> *Type of interview*
> - On the job
>   Clear cut, minor misconduct. Instant verbal censure and indicate organisation limits exceeded.
> - Informal first and subsequent
>   Prior notice of interview date and subject.
> - Formal
>   Prior notice of interview date, subject and relevant paperwork, plus observers.

*Procedure*

The procedure you will follow is very similar for each type of disciplinary interview, with the main difference being the involvement of other people as observers or witnesses.

*Procedure*
- outline subjects for discussion
- recap previous action taken if relevant
- role of observers
- allow interviewee time to explain
- consider interviewee's responses
- joint or interviewer-only solution
- summary, action plan and consequences
- agree review meeting

*Role of observers* This will depend on the disciplinary procedure that your company follows. At a formal interview you will want someone to take notes and possibly to help you keep on track with the interview. The interviewee has the right to bring a colleague or trades union representative if they wish. You all need to be absolutely clear whether this is for silent, moral support or in a speaking role.

In a first, informal, interview it may be more appropriate to hold the discussion between the two of you indicating that unless the situation changes you will initiate more formal procedures. Consult your company policy; it may require observers from the start. Record the interview and have the interviewee sign in case of recurrence.

*Allow interviewee time to explain* The interview enables two-way discussion. There could be many reasons for the interviewee not working or behaving satisfactorily. You need to check that your facts and context are correct giving them plenty of space to explain any extenuating circumstances relevant to the case.

*Consider interviewee's responses* It is possible that, having heard the interviewee's side of the story, you may decide to abandon the disciplinary interview in favour of a discussion about coaching, training or moving into counselling mode.

- Are they entirely to blame?
- Were there mitigating circumstances?
- Is someone else in the company responsible?
- Was there an organisational failure?
- Are these acceptable explanations or excuses?

You may need to adjourn the interview to investigate the new circumstances and to reassess the situation considering the interviewee's statements. You may already have some ideas about the improvements you require but these must be flexible to allow for the interviewee's input. Remember that you are looking for ways to achieve progress rather than dismissal.

*Summary, action plan and consequences* At the end of any disciplinary interview, summarise the discussion and the decisions reached. This ensures that you can check all your points have been covered and can confirm the agreed actions. Divide the action plan into steps to be taken with the required timescale. See that the interviewee has a copy. If other members of staff are to be involved in the action plan they will need written details to follow.

> *Summarise*
> - the subject discussed and why it is not acceptable
> - interviewee's explanation
> - agreed actions and timings
> - next step of discipline if no change

*Agree review meeting* Specify the time limits for the agreed changes and improvement. No further disciplinary action should be necessary during that time unless the interviewee has shown no inclination to change. Hold regular progress checks to monitor behaviour and performance.

If there has been only qualified improvement you may want to increase the time allowed. If the interviewee has made satisfactory improvements it is important that you acknowledge and praise their success.

'We've been discussing your attitude to information requests made over the phone. We have agreed that your responses of swearing and slamming the phone down are not acceptable. I understand that the main problem is having your concentration disturbed and that it takes a long time to reorganise your thoughts.

We have agreed that you will circulate a memo with both our signatures suggesting that telephone enquiries are acceptable before 9.30 and after 16.30. Where this is not possible you would prefer written or electronic mail.

You are going to work at curbing your temper should calls be made outside the requested time.

We have also agreed to meet in a month's time to assess the situation.'

*Notes*
For the on-the-job interview, you can make a brief note to record the fact that you have spoken to the interviewee.

- employee – Jo Smith
- date – 10.03.93
- reason for warning – timekeeping
- your signature

The more formal interviews will require details of the
contents of the interviews and the deadlines for action. Give
a copy to the interviewee as soon as possible after the
interview as well as keeping one on file. Depending on your
company policy, there may be a requirement for you both to
sign and agree as accurate a written record of the interview.

- employee
- date
- reason for interview
- interviewee responses
- actions to be implemented
- timescale
- next step if action not observed/maintained
- signature: interviewee
                interviewer

In the case of an appeal within the company or to an
external arbiter you will need comprehensive notes to show
that you have correctly followed the required procedures.

## Dos and don'ts

*Do*
- ensure no interruptions from people or phones
- convey appropriate formality
- allow for nerves on both sides – offer refreshment
- maintain regular eye contact with interviewee
- avoid raising your voice, physical contact
- keep as relaxed as possible to facilitate listening
- state the issues clearly and specifically with examples
- be consistent in all staff discipline

*Don't*
- get involved in arguments or defensiveness
- use the opportunity to throw every possible complaint at the interviewee
- make personal remarks
- resort to sarcasm

## Checklist

You may not have to conduct many disciplinary interviews, but you should still take time to prepare yourself fully and be aware of your company's procedure just in case you are called upon.

*Key questions*
- Is there a company policy? Do you know it?
- Are you clear about the areas of complaint/ dissatisfaction?
- What evidence can you collect? Where/who from?
- Do you both know which stage of the disciplinary process this is?
- Do either of you require observers?
- Have you listened to the interviewee's points?
- What are the next steps?